Chefs' Special

Marwari Kitchen

Chefs' Special

Marwari Kitchen

Bina Parasramka

Lustre Press
Roli Books

Flavours of Marwari Cooking

Marwaris are people who hail from Rajasthan. They enjoy a rich and spicy cuisine. Rajasthan being a desert, there has always been a dearth of fresh green vegetables. To make up for this, Marwaris have used dehydrated stalks, beans, and berries of various kinds in mouth-watering sweet and spicy preparations. The use of ghee is profuse, as Marwaris believe that it is a primary source of nourishment.

Dal-batti-churma is a speciality of this region. The *panchmela dal* consists of a curry cooked with five different types of dal; *batti* is baked wheat-flour bread dipped in ghee; *churma* is crushed wheat-flour cake mixed with sugar and pistachios.

Preserves such as *bharwan nimbu ka achar* (stuffed lemon pickle), *khatta aam ka achar* (tangy mango pickle) and delightful chutneys are an essential part of the Marwari menu. *Bajra* (maize flour), their staple food, it is available in and around Rajasthan all the year round. *Bajre ki roti* (maize flour bread) with jaggery (*gur*) and *lahsun* (garlic) chutney was what the farmers relished – a combination still loved by the Marwaris.

Cooking is an art, and for people who love to eat and make good food, it can be delightful. Nowadays a lot of stress is laid on food presentation. The use of *varq* (silver leaf), saffron, almonds, and pistachios to decorate desserts is common among the Marwaris. The scent of rose water and saffron in *gulab jamun* enhances its taste. *Badam ka seera* (almond pudding) is made throughout the year in all Marwari homes. Its nutritional value benefits both young and old.

Accompaniments like *kadhi* (yoghurt and gram-flour curry) form a part of the staple diet. *Papads* (pappadum), eaten roasted elsewhere in India, are eaten gravied in Rajasthan. The Marwari community enjoys eating rich food.

As for marriages, it is a matter of days of merry-making, eating, and wearing colourful clothes. Thus, we see Marwari ladies constantly trying to improve and invent new kinds of tasty recipes. They do not, however, leave out the original taste and methods. Some of these recipes are age-old, yet they are greatly relished in homes even today. To make them perfectly is an art and I have tried to guide readers to the best of my ability.

Marwari cuisine is not difficult to cook. And it is crisp, tangy, nutritious, spicy, and wholesome. Just take 100 gm of adventurous spirit, deep-fry in 10 tbsp of enthusiasm, season with a pinch of experimentation and create your own Marwari gourmet delight!

Basic Preparations

Split green gram strips (*mangori*): Take 1¼ cups / 250 gm split green gram (*dhuli moong dal*), soaked for 2 hours, a pinch of asafoetida (*hing*), a 4 ft x 2 ft plastic sheet, and a ½ kg-sized plastic polythene packet.

Drain and grind the split green gram to a smooth and thick consistency. Add the asafoetida and whip together for 2-3 minutes. Grease the plastic sheet lightly on one side. Put some green gram paste in the polythene packet and make a small hole in one corner of the packet. Now press the paste out gradually onto the greased sheet in long thin strands and sun dry. Repeat till all the paste is used up. When it has completely dried, the *mangori* will come off on its own. Store in airtight jars.

Boiled gram flour rounds (*gatta*): Take 2 cups / 200 gm gram flour (*besan*), ½ tsp carom (*ajwain*) seeds, 1 tsp / 2 gm red chilli powder, 2 tbsp / 60 gm yoghurt (*dahi*), 1 tbsp / 15 gm ghee, and salt to taste.

Mix all the ingredients well together. Gradually add water (1 tbsp at a time) and knead to make a stiff dough. Divide the dough equally into lemon-sized portions. Roll each portion out to make a long thin strand of ¼″ diameter. Boil 1½ lt of water in a broad pan. Slowly slide in the strands and boil for about a minute. Drain and leave open for the extra moisture to evaporate. Use as required.

Mustard (*sarson*) Paste: Soak 2 tbsp mustard seeds in 1½ tbsp water for 4-5 hours. Grind to a smooth paste with the water. The paste takes on a white colour when ground finely.

Panch Phoran: Mix equal quantities of fenugreek seeds (*methi dana*), cumin seeds (*jeera*), fennel seeds (*moti saunf*), mustard seeds (*rai*), and onion seeds (*kalonji*). Store in an airtight jar and use as required.

Kair: The dried form of a berry found on desert trees. It is combined with *sangar* as an authentic vegetable preparation. When fresh, it is known as *kairia* and is used to make pickles.

Sangar: This is a bean-like vegetable. Regarded as a delicacy, it is usually stored after it is dried.

Aamras
Sweet mango drink

Beverages

Ingredients:

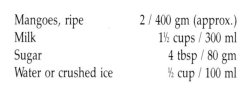

Mangoes, ripe	2 / 400 gm (approx.)
Milk	1½ cups / 300 ml
Sugar	4 tbsp / 80 gm
Water or crushed ice	½ cup / 100 ml

Method:

1. Peel the mangoes and take out the pulp. Discard the skin and the seeds.
2. Blend the pulp with the other ingredients together.
3. Strain and serve chilled.

Note: *This drink tastes best if made of* Gulabkhas *or* Pairee *or* Alphonso *mangoes.*

Kanji
Tangy mustard drink

Beverages

Ingredients:

Red mustard seeds (*rai*), soaked in water for 2 hours	2 tbsp
Red chilli powder	½ tsp / 1 gm
Fennel (*moti saunf*) seeds, coarsely crushed	½ tsp
Yoghurt (*dahi*), thick	1 tsp
Asafoetida (*hing*)	a pinch
Salt to taste	
Water	5 cups / 1 lt

Method:

1. Drain and grind the mustard seeds to a smooth paste.
2. Mix all the ingredients (except water) well for 2-3 minutes in a big bowl.
3. Gradually add the water and mix well.
4. Keep aside to mature overnight. This drink can be preserved for 10-15 days.

Variations: *Parboiled vegetables like potatoes, carrots, cauliflower, and beans can be added to the* kanji, *while just potatoes or carrots also taste good.*

Boiled beetroot cubes, if added, lend colour to the drink. Parboiled black carrot juliennes in red kanji *look and taste wonderful.*

Soft green-gram fritters (moong dal pakories) *in the* kanji *are light to eat.*

10

Kairi Pani
Raw mango appetiser

Preparation time: 15 min.
Cooking time: 5 min.
Makes: 6-8 glasses

B
e
v
e
r
a
g
e
s

Ingredients:

Mangoes, big, raw,	2 / 250 gm
Green coriander relish (*hare dhaneye ki chutney*) (see p. 72)	2 tbsp / 30 gm
Mint (*pudina*) paste	1 tsp / 5 gm
Cumin (*jeera*) seeds, roasted, powdered	1 tsp / 1½ gm
Salt to taste	

Method:

1. Cover the mangoes with enough water and boil in a pressure cooker till very tender.

2. When cool, remove the pulp and discard the seeds. Add 1 lt water to the pulp and mix well. Strain the mixture through a muslin cloth. Discard the pulp.

3. Add the green coriander paste, mint paste, cumin powder, and salt to the strained liquid; mix well. Strain the mixture again. Serve chilled.

Variation: *2 tsp sugar can also be added to this drink it you like it sweet and sour. Salted* boondi *(gram-flour granules) can be added just before serving. This drink is served in small quantities.*

Kesar Shikanji

A refreshing saffron drink

Preparation time: 1 hr.
Cooking time: 15 min.
Makes: 1 lt. concentrate

Ingredients:

Sugar	4 cups / 600 gm
Water	5 cups / 1 lt
Sodium benzoate (class preservative)	a pinch
Lemon (*nimbu*) juice	1 cup / 200 ml
Saffron (*kesar*), soaked in 2 tbsp water for 1 hour	1 tsp / 1 gm

Method:

1. Boil the water and the sugar in a pan, stirring continuously. Cook till the sugar dissolves completely and the syrup is sticky. It should not be too thick or the sugar will set. Remove from heat.
2. Add sodium benzoate and mix well. Keep aside to cool. Add the lemon juice, mix well and then strain the mixture through a thin muslin cloth.
3. Add the soaked saffron, mix well and bottle.

Note: *1 lt of concentrate makes about 20-25 glasses of this refreshing drink.*

Beverages

14

Alu Sabudana Bara

Fried potato and sago cakes

Preparation time: 30 min.
Cooking time: 30 min.
Serves: 8

Snacks and Starters

Ingredients:

Potatoes, boiled, mashed	500 gm
Sago (*sabudana*), soaked for 15 minutes, drained	½ cup / 60 gm
Peanuts (*moongphalli*), coarsely pounded	3⅓ tbsp / 50 gm
Salt to taste	
Ginger (*adrak*), chopped, 1″ piece	1
Green chillies, chopped	2-3
Green coriander (*hara dhaniya*), chopped	2½ tbsp / 10 gm
Lemon (*nimbu*) juice	1
Vegetable oil for deep-frying	

Method:

1. Mix all the ingredients together except the oil and divide the mixture equally into lemon-sized balls.
2. Heat the oil in a wok (*kadhai*); flatten each ball lightly between the palms and fry, a few at a time, till golden. Remove with a slotted spoon and drain the excess oil on paper towels. Repeat till all the balls are fried.
3. Serve hot with *hare dhaniye ki chutney* (see p. 72).

Suhali
Crisp, fried flour savouries

Preparation time: 10 min.
Cooking time: 30 min.
Makes: 20-25 pieces

Ingredients:

Refined flour (*maida*)	2½ cups / 250 gm
Ghee	3 tbsp / 45 gm
Carom seeds (*ajwain*)	½ tsp / 1 gm
Salt	½ tsp / 2 gm
Vegetable oil for deep-frying	

Method:

1. Mix all the ingredients together except the oil and knead into a stiff dough.
2. Divide the dough equally into 20-25 portions. Roll each portion out into a flat disc of 2″ diameter. Pierce each with a fork.
3. Heat the oil in a wok (*kadhai*); fry the discs, a few at a time, on low heat till brown. Remove with a slotted spoon and drain the excess oil on paper towels. Repeat till all the discs are fried.
4. These can be stored for a week in airtight containers and eaten with any pickle of your choice.

Namak Para
Diamond-shaped flour savouries

Preparation time: 20 min.
Cooking time: 30 min.
Makes: 20-25 pieces

Ingredients:

Refined flour (*maida*)	2½ cups / 250 gm
Ghee	3 tbsp / 45 gm
Onion seeds (*kalonji*)	½ tsp / 1 gm
Salt	½ tsp / 2 gm
Vegetable oil for deep-frying	

Method:

1. Mix all the ingredients together except oil and knead. Roll the dough to a ¼"-thick disc.
2. With a sharp knife cut the disc in ½" wide vertical strips.
3. Again cut in a slant about ½"-wide strips to get diamond shapes.
4. Heat the oil in wok (*kadhai*); fry these pieces, a few at a time, on low heat till brown and crisp. Remove with a slotted spoon and drain the excess oil on paper towels. Repeat till all the pieces are fried.
5. This can be stored for a week in airtight containers. Serve with any pickle of your choice.

Moong Dal Ke Chille

Green gram pancakes

Preparation time: 2½ hrs.
Cooking time: 30 min.
Serves: 4-5

Ingredients:

Split green gram (*dhuli moong dal*), soaked for 2 hours	1¼ cups / 250 gm
Ginger (*adrak*), finely chopped, 1" piece	1
Green chillies, finely chopped	2-3
Green coriander (*hara dhaniya*), finely chopped	4 tbsp / 16 gm
Red chilli powder	½ tsp / 1 gm
Cumin (*jeera*) seeds	1 tsp / 1½ gm
Salt to taste	
Vegetable oil for shallow frying	

Method:

1. Drain the green gram and grind to a smooth paste.

2. Add the remaining ingredients except the oil and whip with a ladle for 2-3 minutes to make a semi-thick batter.

3. Heat a griddle (*tawa*); spread 3 tbsp of the batter to make a thin pancake. Add a little oil around the sides. When the underside is done, turn over with the help of a spatula and cook the other side till golden brown. Remove and repeat till all the batter is used up.

4. Serve hot with *hare dhaniye ki chutney* (see p. 72).

Note: *The green gram batter can be refrigerated for a few days but the pancakes should be made just before serving.*

Matar Gujiya
Stuffed green pea patties

Preparation time: 1 hr.
Cooking time: 40 min.
Makes: 25 pieces

Ingredients:

Refined flour (*maida*)	5 cups / 500 gm
Ghee	6 tbsp / 90 gm
For the filling:	
Ghee	2 tbsp / 30 gm
Cumin (*jeera*) seeds	1 tsp / 2 gm
Ginger, chopped, 1" piece	1
Green chillies, chopped	3-4
Green peas (*hara matar*), boiled	400 gm
Salt to taste	
Black salt (*kala namak*)	½ tsp / 2 gm
Cumin (*jeera*) seeds, roasted, powdered	1 tsp / 1½ gm
Chaat masala	1 tsp / 2 gm

Vegetable oil for deep-frying

Method:

1. Sift the flour and rub in the ghee. Knead with enough water to make a stiff dough. Cover with a moist cloth and keep aside.

2. **For the filling,** heat the ghee in a wok (*kadhai*); add the powdered cumin seeds, ginger, and green chillies; sauté for 2-3 seconds. Add the green peas, salt, black salt, cumin powder, and *chaat* masala; sauté for 4-5 minutes.

3. When the mixture is dry enough, remove the wok from the heat and transfer the mixture on a flat dish to cool.

4. Divide the dough equally into 25 portions. Roll each out into a small disc of 3" diameter. Put 1 tbsp

filling in the centre of one disc and fold over to make a half circle. Press the edges well together to seal the filling inside. With a fork press the edges again. Repeat till all the patties are done.

5. Heat the oil in a wok (*kadhai*); fry the patties, a few at a time, on medium heat till brown and crisp. Remove with a slotted spoon and drain the excess oil on paper towels.

6. Serve hot with *imli ki chutney* (see p. 68) or *hare dhaniye ki chutney* (see p. 72).

Fresh & Green
After boiling the green peas,
pour cold water over them so that
they remain fresh and green.

Doodh Ka Bhutta

Corn cooked in milk

Preparation time: 10 min.
Cooking time: 20 min.
Serves: 6

Ingredients:

Corn (*bhutta*) kernels, crushed	250 gm
Milk	1¼ cups / 250 ml
Butter	1½ tbsp / 30 gm
Salt	½ tsp / 2 gm
White pepper (*safed mirch*) powder	¼ tsp / 1 gm

Method:

1. Mix the crushed corn with the milk and bring to a boil. Cook, stirring constantly, till the mixture thickens.

2. Add the remaining ingredients; mix well. Remove from heat and serve as a topping on toast or as a stuffing in grilled sandwiches.

Sangar Ka Saag

A Marwari delicacy

Preparation time: 20 min. + overnight
Cooking time: 15 min.
Serves: 8-10

Ingredients:

Sangar (see p. 7)	150 gm
Kair (see p. 7)	30 gm
Dry red chillies (*sookhi lal mirch*)	10-12
Mangoes, raw, dried, cut into strips	8-10 pieces
Mustard seeds (*rai*)	5 tbsp / 45 gm
Lotus stems (*kamal kakri*), washed thoroughly, cut into thin rounds	2 pieces
Turmeric (*haldi*) powder	2 tsp / 4 gm
Salt	5-6 tsp / 20-30 gm
Red chilli powder	4 tsp / 8 gm
Mango powder (*amchoor*)	2 tsp / 4 gm
Vegetable / mustard oil	¾ cup / 150 ml
Cumin (*jeera*) seeds	2 tsp / 3 gm

Method:

1. Soak the *sangar* overnight in a big bowl containing lots of water, 1 tsp oil, 1 tsp salt and 1 tsp turmeric powder. Drain.
2. Clean and soak these ingredients separately overnight: *kair*, dry red chillies, mango strips, and mustard seeds. Drain.
3. Cover the *sangar* and *kair* with enough water and boil till soft. Drain.
4. Grind the mustard seeds to a smooth paste.
5. Mix the boiled *sangar-kair* mixture with the lotus stems, dry red chillies, mango strips, mustard paste, turmeric powder, and salt in a big bowl.
6. Dilute the red chilli powder and mango powder in 1 cup water.

7. Heat the oil in a wok (*kadhai*) till it starts smoking. Cool slightly and then add the cumin seeds. Gradually add the diluted spices.

8. Remove from heat, add the *sangar* mixture and mix well. Leave to mature for a day.

Note: *This is ready to eat only after the mustard paste matures a little. It can be preserved for 10-15 days.*

≈

Prevent Sp(oil)ing the Floor
Spilt oil can be easily cleaned up by spreading newspapers over it. These absorb the liquid. Use a wet rag to complete the cleaning.

≈

Kathi Dal
Tangy split green gram

Preparation time: 30 min.
Cooking time: 20 min.
Serves: 6-7

Ingredients:

Split green gram (*dhuli moong dal*), soaked
    for 30 minutes, drained   1 cup / 200 gm
Ghee   2 tbsp / 30 gm
Cumin (*jeera*) seeds   ½ tsp
Asafoetida (*hing*)   a pinch
Turmeric (*haldi*) powder   ½ tsp / 1 gm
Salt to taste
Water   3 cups / 600 ml

Method:

1. Heat the ghee in a pressure cooker; add the cumin seeds and asafoetida. When the seeds start spluttering add the split green gram. Sauté for 2 minutes.
2. Add turmeric powder, salt and 3 cups water. Mix well and close the pressure cooker. Cook till 3 whistles. Remove from heat and allow the pressure to release slowly.
3. Mix the green gram mixture with a ladle and serve hot with steamed rice.

Alu Bhujee
Smoked potatoes

Preparation time: 15 min.
Cooking time: 2-3 min
Serves: 2-3

Ingredients:

Potato, big, boiled, mashed coarsely	1
Red chilli powder	¼ tsp
Green coriander (*hara dhaniya*), finely chopped	1 tsp
Salt to taste	
A small piece of wood coal	

Method:

1. Mix all the ingredients (except the wood coal) lightly in a bowl.
2. Light the coal till it is red. Place the lighted coal in the centre of the potato mixture; add a dash of ghee and cover immediately for 2-3 minutes.
3. Remove the coal, mix lightly and serve.

Variations: *The same process can be followed with other food items such as roasted and crushed pappadums* (papad)*, lightly pounded berries* (kair)*, boiled and stringed cluster beans* (guar ki phalli)*. Other vegetables can also be smoked in the same way.*

Vegetarian

Alu Dum

Fried potatoes coated with thick tomato gravy

Preparation time: I hr.
Cooking time: 40-50 min.
Serves: 4-5

Ingredients:

Potatoes, small, peeled, fried till golden and tender	500 gm
Tomatoes	3-4 / 300 gm
Red chilli powder	2 tsp / 4 gm
Garlic (*lasan*) cloves	3-4
Cinnamon (*dalchini*), 1″ stick	1
Cloves (*laung*)	1
Green cardamoms (*choti elaichi*)	5
Vegetable oil	4 tbsp / 60 ml
Sugar	¼ tsp
Onions, big, grated	2
Ginger (*adrak*), grated, 2″ piece	1
Salt to taste	
Water	½ cup / 100 ml

Method:

1. Boil the tomatoes till soft. When cool, peel and blend to make a purée. Add red chilli powder and 1 tbsp oil; mix well and keep aside.
2. Crush the garlic, cinnamon stick, cloves, and green cardamoms together.
3. Heat the oil in a wok (*kadhai*); add sugar, crushed garlic mixture, onions, and ginger; sauté till golden brown. Add the tomato purée; sauté till the mixture leaves the sides of the wok.
4. Add the fried potatoes and salt; sauté again. Add the water, mix and cook covered, on low heat, for 3-4 minutes. The gravy should be thick enough to coat the potatoes.
5. Serve hot garnished with green coriander.

Mogar
Dry and spicy green gram

Preparation time: 30 min.
Cooking time: 20 min.
Serves: 6-8

Vegetarian

Ingredients:

Split green gram (*dhuli moong dal*), soaked for 30 minutes	1¼ cups / 250 gm
Ghee	4 tbsp / 60 gm
Cumin (*jeera*) seeds	½ tsp
Asafoetida (*hing*)	a pinch
Bay leaves (*tej patta*)	1-2
Turmeric (*haldi*) powder	½ tsp / 1 gm
Red chilli powder	1 tsp / 2 gm
Salt	I tsp / 4 gm
Coriander (*dhaniya*) powder	2 tsp / 3 gm
Garam masala	½ tsp / 1 gm
Mango powder (*amchoor*)	1 tsp / 2 gm
Sugar	½ tsp / 1½ gm

Method:

1. Heat the ghee in a wok (*kadhai*); add the cumin seeds, asafoetida, and bay leaves. When they start spluttering, add the turmeric powder and red chilli powder; sauté for a few minutes. Add ½ cup water, mix well.

2. Add the drained green gram, salt, coriander powder, and 1 cup water, stir occasionally, and cook till the mixture is completely dry.

3. Before removing from heat, add garam masala, mango powder, and sugar. Mix lightly and serve.

Bharwan Parwal

Stuffed parwar

Preparation time: 10 min.
Cooking time: 10 min.
Serves: 4-6

Vegetarian

Ingredients:

Parwar (*parwal*), medium, peeled, slit vertically	10
For the stuffing:	
Red chilli powder	½ tsp / 1 gm
Coriander (*dhaniya*) powder	¾ tsp / 1 gm
Mango powder (*amchoor*)	½ tsp / 1 gm
Turmeric (*haldi*) powder	¼ tsp / ½ gm
Garam masala (optional)	¼ tsp / ½ gm
Salt to taste	
Ghee	1 tbsp / 15 gm
Cumin (*jeera*) seeds	1 tsp / 1½ gm

Method:

1. **For the stuffing**, mix all the ingredients together. Add 3-4 drops of ghee to bind the mixture. Stuff 1 tsp filling into each parwar.

2. Heat the ghee in a pressure pan; add the cumin seeds. When they splutter, add the stuffed parwars. Any leftover stuffing can be sprinkled over the parwars. Add 2 tbsp of water, cover the pan and cook till 2 whistles.

3. Release the pressure immediately to retain the colour of the parwars. Serve hot.

Panchmela Dal

Five-in-one pulse delight

Vegetarian

Ingredients:

Split green gram (*dhuli moong dal*)	30 gm
Whole green gram (*chilka moong*)	40 gm
Bengal gram (*chana dal*)	40 gm
Split red gram (*arhar dal*)	30 gm
Black gram (*urad dal*)	30 gm
Dried pea (*matar dal*)	30 gm
Ghee	4 tbsp / 60 gm
Asafoetida (*hing*)	a big pinch
Cumin (*jeera*) seeds	1½ tsp / 3 gm
Ginger (*adrak*), julienned	1½" piece
Bay leaves (*tej patta*)	2-3
Coriander (*dhaniya*) powder	1 tsp / 1½ gm
Mango powder (*amchoor*)	1 tsp / 2 gm
Tomato, big	1
Water	3 cups / 600 ml
Salt	2 tsp / to taste
Turmeric (*haldi*) powder	1 tsp / 2 gm
Red chilli powder	1 tsp / 2 gm
Sugar	a pinch
Green coriander (*hara dhaniya*), chopped	5 tbsp / 20 gm
Green chilli, slit	1

Method:

1. Soak all the pulses together for half an hour. Drain and keep aside.

2. Heat 2 tbsp ghee in a pressure cooker; add asafoetida, cumin seeds, ginger, and bay leaves; sauté. Add the pulses and stir-fry for 2-3 minutes.

3. Add coriander powder, mango powder, and tomato; sauté again for 2-3 minutes.

4. Add water, salt, turmeric powder and pressure cook till 3 whistles; then allow the pressure to release by itself.

5. Heat 2 tbsp ghee in a small pan; add the red chilli powder mixed with 3 tbsp water and sugar. Lower heat and simmer for 1 minute to get a rich red colour.

6. Add this, green coriander and the green chilli to the cooked pulses. Mix well and serve hot.

Note: *Split red gram* (arhar dal) *can be made in the same way.*

≈

Insect-Free Pulses

*To prevent insects from attacking pulses
clean and rub a little oil on the pulses
before storing them in airtight containers.*

≈

Gatte Ka Saag Dahiwala

Gram flour strips in yoghurt curry

Preparation time: 20 min.
Cooking time: 10 min.
Serves: 5-6

Ingredients:

Gatta (see p. 6),	
cut into ¼" pieces	250 gm
Yoghurt (*dahi*)	2 cups / 400 gm
Ghee	2 tbsp / 30 gm
Asafoetida (*hing*)	a pinch
Cumin (*jeera*) seeds	½ tsp
Ginger (*adrak*), chopped	1 tsp / 10 gm
Red chilli powder	1 tsp / 2 gm
Turmeric (*haldi*) powder	½ tsp / 1 gm
Salt to taste	
Green coriander (*hara dhaniya*),	
finely chopped	1 tbsp / 4 gm

Method:

1. Strain the yoghurt through a muslin cloth. Add ½ cup water and mix well.
2. Add the gram flour strips; mix well.
3. Heat the ghee in a wok (*kadhai*); add asafoetida, cumin seeds, ginger, red chilli powder, and turmeric powder. When the seeds start spluttering, immediately add the yoghurt mixture. Bring the mixture to the boil, stirring constantly.
4. Add salt and mix well. Lower heat and simmer for 2-3 minutes.
5. Serve hot garnished with green coriander.

Kadhi
Yoghurt and gram flour curry

Preparation time: 10 min.
Cooking time: 10 min.
Serves: 5-6

Vegetarian

Ingredients:

Yoghurt (*dahi*), sour	1¼ cups / 250 gm
Gram flour (*besan*)	1½ tbsp / 15 gm
Water	1 cup / 200 ml
Salt	1 tsp / to taste
Turmeric (*haldi*) powder	¼ tsp
For the tempering:	
Ghee	1 tbsp / 15 gm
Asafoetida (*hing*)	a pinch
Bay leaves (*tej patta*)	2-3
Mustard seeds (*rai*)	½ tsp / 1½ gm
Dry red chillies (*sookhi lal mirch*)	2-3
Red chilli powder, diluted in 1 tbsp water	¼ tsp

Method:

1. Mix together the gram flour, yoghurt, and water thoroughly; strain. Add salt and turmeric powder, bring the mixture to the boil stirring constantly. Cook on low heat for 2-3 minutes.

2. **For the tempering**, heat the ghee in a small pan; add all the ingredients except the red chilli water. Sauté for a few seconds. Now add the diluted red chilli powder; simmer for 2-3 seconds.

3. Mix this with the gram flour mixture. Serve hot with steamed rice.

Variations: *You can add finely diced boiled mixed vegetables or thin slices of* gatta *(see p. 6) or gram flour fritters* (besan ke pakories) *or boiled* mangori *(see p. 6).*

Rajasthani Panchmela
Mixed vegetables – Rajasthani style

Preparation time: 45 min.
Cooking time: 30 min.
Serves: 5-6

I n g r e d i e n t s :

Cauliflower (*phool gobi*), small, cut into florets	1
White radish (*safed mooli*), medium, peeled, cut into ½″ cubes	2
Cucumber (*khira*), peeled, cut into ½″ cubes	1
Bottle gourd (*lauki*), small, peeled, cut into ½″ cubes	1
Parwar (*parwal*), peeled, cut into ½″ cubes	6-7
Red pumpkin (*lal kaddu*), peeled, cut into ½″ cubes	250 gm
Spinach (*palak*), chopped	200 gm
Tomatoes, finely chopped	200 gm
Capsicum (*Shimla mirch*), finely chopped	200 gm
Vegetable oil	4 tbsp / 60 ml
Panch phoran (see p. 7)	1 tbsp
Ginger (*adrak*), julienned, 1½″ piece	1
Green chillies, slit	5-6
Salt to taste	
Turmeric (*haldi*) powder	1 tsp / 2 gm
Red chilli powder	1 tsp / 2 gm
Mango powder (*amchoor*)	1 tsp / 2 gm
Garam masala	1 tsp / 2 gm

M e t h o d :

1. Heat the oil in a wok (*kadhai*); add the *panch phoran*, ginger, and green chillies; sauté for a minute. Add all the vegetables except the tomatoes and capsicum.

2. Add salt and turmeric powder. Cook covered, on low heat, till the vegetables are well done. Add the tomatoes, capsicum, red chilli powder, and mango powder; sauté for 2-3 minutes till well mixed.

3. Remove the wok from the heat, add the garam masala, mix well and serve hot.

Cool-n'-Digest

*Soak the cucumber in salt water
for about an hour or two before using.
This will make it more digestible.*

Patli Mangori

Green gram pieces in tomato gravy

Preparation time: 40 min.
Cooking time: 20 min.
Serves: 3-4

Ingredients:

Mangori (see p. 6), coarsely crushed	200 gm
Ghee	2 tbsp / 30 gm
Asafoetida (*hing*)	a pinch
Cumin (*jeera*) seeds	½ tsp
Ginger (*adrak*), finely chopped, 1″ piece	1
Green chilli, slit	1
Salt to taste	
Turmeric (*haldi*) powder	¼ tsp
Water	1½ cups / 300 ml
Tomato, big, chopped	1
Red chilli powder	1 tsp / 2 gm
Mango powder (*amchoor*)	½ tsp / 1 gm
Green coriander (*hara dhaniya*), chopped	1 tbsp / 4 gm

Method:

1. Heat the ghee in a wok (*kadhai*); add the asafoetida, cumin seeds, ginger, and green chilli. Add the *mangori* and sauté for 2 minutes. Add salt, turmeric powder, and water. Bring the mixture to the boil, lower heat and simmer till the *mangori* is tender.
2. Increase the flame, add the remaining ingredients (except green coriander). Boil till the gravy is smooth and thick.
3. Serve hot garnished with green coriander.

Variations: *For* palak mangori *add 100 gm of boiled and crushed spinach (omit green coriander) to the boiling* mangori. *Mix well, remove from heat immediately and serve hot with* besan *or* bajre ki roti *(see p. 57).*

Batti

Baked wheat flour bread dipped in ghee

Preparation time: 1 hr.
Cooking time: 20 min.
Serves: 6-8

Accompaniments

Ingredients:

Wholewheat flour (*atta*)	4 cups / 400 gm
Ghee	3½ tbsp / 52 gm
Salt	1 tsp / 4 gm
Sugar	½ tsp / 1½ gm
Bicarbonate of soda	½ tsp / 3 gm

Ghee to dip the *batti* in before serving

Method:

1. Sift the wholewheat flour, rub in 3 tbsp ghee. Add salt, sugar, and bicarbonate of soda.
2. Knead with approximately ¾ cup water into a hard dough. Cover the dough with a moist cloth and keep aside for 1 hour.
3. Divide the dough equally into lemon-sized portions. Shape each into smooth rounds with your palms and steam for 20 minutes in an electrical steamer or in a pressure cooker (without the whistle).
4. Now roast them on a coal fire or in a *tandoor* till they are well done. Wipe with a clean cloth, dip in hot ghee and serve immediately with *panchmela dal* (see p. 38).

Variations: *To make stuffed* batti, *make a filling of gram flour, carom seeds* (ajwain), *red chilli powder, and salt with a little water. Make a hollow in the centre of each round and stuff in this filling. Smoothen each round before steaming.*

Matar Ki Puri

Shallow fried bread stuffed with green peas

Preparation time: 30 min.
Cooking time: 30 min.
Makes: 15

Ingredients:

Refined four (*maida*)	3 cups / 300 gm
Vegetable oil	2 tbsp / 30 ml

For the filling:

Green peas (*matar*), shelled, ground to a smooth paste	400 gm
Ghee	2-3 tbsp / 30-45 gm
Asafoetida (*hing*)	a pinch
Salt to taste	
Sugar	½ tsp / 1½ gm
Bicarbonate of soda	a pinch

Method:

1. **For the filling**, heat the ghee in a pan; add all the ingredients and sauté till the mixture leaves the sides of the wok and is not sticky to touch. Remove and divide the mixture into 15 portions.

2. Rub 1 tbsp oil into the refined flour and knead with enough water into a soft dough. Divide the dough equally into 15 portions.

3. Take a portion of the dough, make a hollow in the centre and fill a portion of the green-pea mixture. Fold over the edges to seal the filling inside. Repeat till all are done. Cover the stuffed balls with a moist cloth and keep aside for 10-15 minutes.

4. With the help of dry flour, roll out each ball into a thin disc of 10″ diameter.

5. Roast the disc on a griddle (*tawa*) on both sides using 1½ tsp oil. Remove and repeat with the other discs. Cover with aluminium foil.

Moong Dal Puri

Stuffed green gram bread

Preparation time: 2½ hrs.
Cooking time: 30 min.
Makes: 12-13

Ingredients:

Refined flour (*maida*)	2¼ cups / 250 gm
Vegetable oil	3 tbsp / 45 ml
Asafoetida (*hing*)	a pinch
Cumin (*jeera*) seeds	½ tsp
Split green gram (*dhuli moong dal*), soaked for 2 hours, drained and ground to a paste	1 cup / 200 gm
Red chilli powder	2 tbsp
Salt to taste	
Garam masala	1 tsp / 2 gm

Method:

1. Heat 2 tbsp oil in a pan; add asafoetida and cumin seeds, sauté for a few seconds. Add the green gram paste, and the remaining ingredients; sauté till the mixture leaves the sides of the pan and is soft.

2. Rub 1 tbsp oil into the refined flour and knead with enough water into a soft dough. Divide the dough equally into 12-13 portions.

3. Take a portion, make a hollow in the centre and fill with the green gram mixture. Seal the filling inside. Repeat with the other portions. Cover the stuffed balls with a moist cloth and keep aside for 10-15 minutes. Roll out each portion into a thin disc of 10″ diameter with some dry flour.

4. Roast the disc on a griddle (*tawa*) on both sides with 1½ tsp oil. Remove and repeat with the other discs. Cover with aluminum foil. They can be eaten cold with *sangar ka saag* (see p. 26).

Tai Roti
Shallow fried cottage cheese bread

Preparation time: 30 min.
Cooking time: 45 min.
Makes: 20

I n g r e d i e n t s :

Refined flour (*maida*)	5 cups / 500 gm
Cottage cheese (*paneer*), grated	200 gm
Cabbage (*bandh gobi*), grated	200 gm
Capsicum (*Shimla mirch*), big, grated	1
Salt to taste	
Milk	1 cup / 200 ml
Ghee to shallow fry	

M e t h o d :

1. Mix the flour with the cottage cheese, cabbage, capsicum, and salt.
2. Add the milk gradually and knead into a stiff dough.
3. Divide the dough equally into 20 portions and roll each out to make a small disc of 4" diameter.
4. Heat a griddle (*tawa*); lay a disc flat on it and roast both the sides, till half done. The half done discs can be kept for 5-6 hours.
5. Before serving, shallow fry the discs on a griddle till golden and crisp. The discs can be roasted on a coal fire or in a *tandoor*. To avoid the use of ghee.

Variation: *Instead of cottage cheese, cabbage and capsicum the following combinations can be used in the above method:*
* *Coarsely crushed potatoes, green peas, and cauliflower;*
* *Finely chopped fenugreek leaves;*
* *Chopped spinach and finely diced onions;*
* *Coarsely crushed carrots, beans and green peas.*

Missi Roti

Spicy gram flour bread

Preparation time: 30 min.
Cooking time: 30 min.
Makes: 15

A c c o m p a n i m e n t s

Ingredients:

Wholewheat flour (*atta*)	2¼ cups / 250 gm
Gram flour (*besan*)	2¼ cups / 250 gm
Yoghurt (*dahi*), hung in a muslin cloth	½ cup / 100 gm
Carom seeds (*ajwain*)	1 tsp / 2 gm
Red chilli powder	1 tsp / 2 gm
Cumin (*jeera*) seeds	½ tsp
Salt to taste	
Ghee	2 tbsp / 30 gm

Method:

1. Mix all the ingredients accept ghee in a large bowl.

2. Knead with a little water, at a time, into a semi-soft dough.

3. Divide the dough into 15 portions and roll each out to a 4″ diameter disc.

4. Heat a griddle (*tawa*); roast the disc evenly on both sides. Now remove the griddle from the flame and roast the disc directly on the flame on both sides till well done but not burnt. Remove and repeat with the other discs.

5. Smear 1 tsp ghee on each disc and serve hot.

Variations: *Finely chopped spinach or fenugreek leaves can be added to the dough, to give colour to the* missi roti.

Bajre Ki Roti
Millet flour bread

Preparation time: 20 min.
Cooking time: 20 min.
Serves: 6-8

Ingredients:

Millet flour (*bajre ka atta*)	5 cups / 500 gm
Salt	a pinch
Ghee	6-7 tbsp / 90-105 gm
Coal fire to roast the *roti*	

Method:

1. Sift the millet flour and salt together. Gradually add enough warm water and knead with greased palms to make a semi-soft dough. Knead the dough 5 minutes before making the *roti*.

2. Divide the dough equally into lemon-sized portions. Flatten each portion with your palms, pressing the edges together, and make 5-6″ diameter discs (they should be slightly thick). This has to be done carefully so that the edges do not break. Avoid using the rolling pin.

3. Heat a griddle (*tawa*); lay a disc flat on it and roast both sides. Then put it directly on a coal fire to make it crisp. Smear 2 tbsp ghee on the disc, crumple lightly between both palms and serve hot. Repeat with the other discs.

4. Serve immediately with yoghurt, jaggery, onion, and *lahsun* chutney (see p. 70) or *sangar ka saag* (see p. 26).

Urad Kachori

Fried bread with black gram

Preparation time: 3 hrs.
Cooking time: 30 min.
Makes: 20

Accompaniments

Ingredients:

Black gram (*urad dal*), soaked for 1½ hours	⅔ cup / 100 gm
Refined flour (*maida*)	2 cups / 200 gm
Semolina (*suji*)	1 cup / 150 gm
Asafoetida (*hing*)	a pinch
Onion seeds (*kalonji*)	½ pinch
Salt to taste	
Vegetable oil	1½ tbsp / 22 ml

Method:

1. Drain the black gram and grind to a smooth paste.
2. Mix the black gram paste with the remaining ingredients. Add a little water and knead to make a soft dough. Keep aside for 1 hour.
3. Before frying, knead the dough again with well-greased palms and on a well-greased table top. divide the dough into lemon-sized balls. Roll each ball out carefully into a 5″ diameter disc.
4. Heat the oil in a wok (*kadhai*); fry the discs, one by one, turning them over frequently, on high heat till golden. They will be slightly white on the edges. Remove with a slotted spoon and drain the excess oil on paper towels.
5. Serve hot with *alu dum* (see p. 32).

Gobi Matar Ke Chawal

Cauliflower and pea pilaf

Preparation time: 45 min.
Cooking time: 15 min.
Serves: 4

Ingredients:

Basmati rice, soaked for 30 minutes, drained	¾ cup / 150 gm
Cauliflower (*phool gobi*), cut into florets	15
Green peas (*matar*)	100 gm
Ghee	2 tbsp / 30 gm
Bay leaves (*tej patta*)	2
Cumin (*jeera*) seeds	½ tsp
Turmeric (*haldi*) powder	¼ tsp
Salt to taste	
Garam masala	¼ tsp
Water, hot	1½ cups / 300 ml

Method:

1. Heat the ghee in a pressure cooker; add the bay leaves, cumin seeds, turmeric powder, rice, and salt; sauté for 2-3 minutes.
2. Add garam masala and hot water; mix well and bring to the boil. Add the vegetables and close the pressure cooker.
3. After 2 whistles release the pressure and transfer the *pulao* onto a serving platter.
4. Serve hot.

Variation: *If onion is used, sauté the finely chopped onion, before adding the rice; do not use turmeric powder for a brown vegetable* pilaf. *Any other vegetable* pilaf *can be prepared in the same way.*

Kanika Bhog

Green gram and rice preparation

Preparation time: 1 hr
Cooking time: 10 min.
Serves: 4-5

Accompaniments

Ingredients:

Rice, soaked for 1 hour, drained	¾ cup / 150 gm
Split green gram (*dhuli moong dal*), soaked for 1 hour, drained	2½ tbsp / 50 gm
Ghee	2 tbsp / 30 gm
Black cardamoms (*badi elaichi*)	2
Cloves (*laung*)	4
Salt	1 tsp / 4 gm
Sugar	3 tsp / 9 gm
Raisins (*kishmish*)	10-12
Water	2 cups / 400 ml

Method:

1. Heat the ghee in a pressure pan; add the black cardamoms and cloves; sauté for a while.
2. Add the remaining ingredients; mix well. Close the pan and cook till 2 whistles. Remove the pan from the heat.
3. After 2-3 minutes release the pressure; mix gently and serve hot.

Dahi Bhat

Yoghurt rice with vegetables

Preparation time: 15 min.
Cooking time: 25 min.
Serves: 4

Ingredients:

Rice	1 cup / 200 gm
Mixed vegetables, finely chopped	1 cup
Yoghurt (*dahi*), hung for 2 hours	1 cup / 200 gm
Salt to taste	
Ghee	1 tbsp / 15 gm
Mustard seeds (*rai*)	½ tsp / 1 gm
Curry leaves (*kadhi patta*)	4-5

Method:

1. Boil the rice, drain the water and keep aside.
2. Boil the vegetables till tender, drain and mix with the boiled rice. Keep aside to cool.
3. Add the yoghurt and salt; mix gently.
4. Heat the ghee in a wok (*kadhai*); add the mustard seeds and curry leaves; sauté for a few seconds. Add the rice mixture; sauté for 2 minutes and serve warm.

Dahi Pakori

Fried pulse dumplings in yoghurt

Preparation time: 2½ hrs.
Cooking time: 20 min.
Serves: 5-6

Ingredients:

For the *pakoris*:

Split green gram (*dhuli moong dal*)	½ cup / 80 gm
Black gram (*urad dal*)	½ cup / 80 gm
Ginger (*adrak*), grated, 1" piece	1
Bicarbonate of soda	a pinch
Salt to taste	
Vegetable oil for frying	
Yoghurt (*dahi*), strained	2½ cups / 500 gm
Salt to taste	
Red chilli powder	1 tsp / 2 gm
Cumin (*jeera*) seeds, roasted, powdered	1 tsp / 1½ gm
Tamarind chutney (see p. 68)	100 gm
Green coriander relish (see p. 72)	2 tbsp

Method:

1. **For the *pakoris*,** After soaking the green and black grams for 2 hours grind to a smooth paste. Add the remaining ingredients. Whip till the batter is smooth, and of dropping consistency.

2. Heat the oil in a pan; carefully drop tablespoonfuls of the batter into the hot oil. Fry till golden brown. Remove with a slotted spoon and immerse the dumplings in salted water for 5-7 minutes. Repeat till all the batter is used up.

3. Remove the soaked dumplings; squeeze out the excess water and arrange them in a bowl.

4. Mix the salt with the yoghurt and pour over the dumplings. Sprinkle the spices, tamarind and green coriander relish; serve.

Hari Mirch Ka Achar

Stuffed green chilli pickle

Preparation time: 20 min.
Making time: 4-5 days

Ingredients:

Green chillies, long and thick	1 kg
For the filling:	
Salt	200 gm
Mustard seeds (*rai*), powdered	200 gm
Turmeric (*haldi*) powder	1½ tsp / 3 gm
Aniseed (*saunf*), coarsely pounded	1½ tbsp
Onion seeds (*kalonji*)	½ tsp / ¾ gm
Asafoetida (*hing*)	a pinch
Lemon (*nimbu*) juice	5

Method:

1. Wash and wipe dry the green chillies. Make a vertical slit in the centre of each chilli.
2. **For the filling,** mix all the spices together. Add the lemon juice and mix well again.
3. Fill each chilli with a generous amount of this mixture. Store the stuffed chillies in an opaque jar and keep in the sun for 4-5 days. Shake the jar twice every day.
4. The chillies will become softer as the days go by, but can be consumed as soon as the filling sticks to the chillies.

Note: *Do not use a glass jar to store this pickle as the green chillies get discoloured.*

Imli Ki Chutney
Tamarind chutney

A c c o m p a n i m e n t s

Ingredients:

Tamarind (*imli*)	100 gm
Jaggery (*gur*)	200 gm
Black salt (*kala namak*)	1½ tsp / 6 gm
Salt	2 tsp / 8 gm
Cumin (*jeera*) seeds, roasted, powdered	1½ tsp / 3 gm
Green cardamoms (*choti elaichi*) powdered	4-5
Ginger powder (*sonth*)	½ tsp / 1 gm

Method:

1. Soak the tamarind and jaggery together for 4-5 hours.
2. Mash the two thoroughly with a wooder spoon or rub between your palms. Strain through a muslin cloth.
3. Add the remaining ingredients and bring the mixture to a boil stirring continuously.
4. Cool and preserve.

Note: *If refrigerated, this can stay for about 15-20 days.*

(Photographs on facing page: **top:** *Dahi Mirch;* **bottom left:** *Lahsun Chutney;* **bottom right:** *Imli Ki Chutney)*

Lahsun Chutney
Garlic relish

Preparation time: 10 min.
Cooking time: 2-3 min.

Ingredients:

Garlic (*lasan*), thick cloves	15-16
Red chilli powder	2 tbsp
White vinegar (*sirka*)	4 tbsp / 60 ml
Salt to taste	
Vegetable oil	5 tbsp / 75 ml

Method:

1. Mix all the ingredients together except the oil and blend to a smooth paste.
2. Heat the oil in a pan; sauté the garlic paste for 2-3 minutes. Remove the pan from the heat.
3. Cool and preserve.

Smart Garlic

When you buy garlic heads, see that they are small, compact and heavy in the hand. Reject the light ones.

Dahi Mirch

Crushed green chillies blended in yoghurt

Preparation time: 5 min.
Cooking time: 10 min.

Ingredients:

Yoghurt (*dahi*), strained   1 cup / 200 gm
Green chillies   10-12
Mustard (*sarson*) oil   4 tbsp / 60 ml
Prepared mustard (see p. 6)
    or *kasundi*   2 tbsp / 30 gm
Salt to taste

Method:

1. Boil the green chillies and crush them coarsely.
2. Blend all the ingredients together with a hand mixer for 3-4 seconds.
3. Store in an airtight jar and keep in a cool, dry place. The chillies will be good for up to 8-10 days.

Comfort Snip

*Cut green chillies with a pair of
scissors to avoid the burning
sensation on your fingers.*

Hare Dhaniye Ki Chutney
Green coriander relish

Ingredients:

Green coriander (*hara dhaniya*) 4 cups / 100 gm	
Green chillies	2
Ginger (*adrak*), 1" piece	1
Garlic (*lasan*), cloves (optional)	2
Cumin (*jeera*) seeds	½ tsp
Lemon (*nimbu*) juice	1

Method:

1. Blend all the ingredients except the lemon juice to a smooth paste.
2. Store the relish in a dry glass jar, in the refrigerator.
3. Just before serving, add the lemon juice, mix well and serve as an accompaniment.

Note: *If garlic is used then omit cumin seeds.*

Bharwan Nimbu Ka Achar

Lemon stuffed with black pepper

Preparation time: 20 min.
Making time: 1 week

Ingredients:

Lemons (*nimbu*)	30

For the filling:

Pink rock salt (*halke rang ka kala namak*), powdered	125 gm
Black peppercorns (*sabut kali mirch*), powdered	70 gm
Asafoetida (*hing*), roasted	¼ tsp / 1¼ gm
Sugar, powdered	1 cup / 150 gm

Method:

1. Squeeze the juice of 5 lemons. Keep aside. Wash and wipe dry the rest of the lemons. Slit each lemon crosswise. They should be joint at the base.
2. **For the filling**, mix all the ingredients together and fill each lemon with this mixture.
3. Put the stuffed lemons in a glass jar and top with the lemon juice. Keep the jar in the sun for a few days till the lemons become soft.
4. When soft, add the sugar and mix well. Keep in the sun again for 4-5 days.

Kairi Ki Kesaria Launji

Mango-saffron chutney with dry fruits

Ingredients:

Mangoes, raw, peeled, grated into thick strands	250 gm
Sugar	1⅓ cups / 200 gm
Saffron (*kesar*), diluted	1 tsp / 1 gm
Pistachios (*pista*), blanched, chopped	1¼ tbsp / 20 gm
Almonds (*badam*), blanched, chopped	1¼ tbsp / 20 gm
Salt	a pinch

Method:

1. Squeeze out the excess liquid from the grated mangoes. Add the sugar, mix well and keep aside for 20-25 minutes.

2. When the sugar dissolves completely, cook the mixture in a pan, on low heat, till the mangoes become soft and the syrup sticky enough to hold together. Remove the pan from the heat. Keep aside to cool.

3. Now add the saffron, pistachios, almonds, and salt; mix well and serve as an accompaniment with any fried snack.

Khatta Aam Ka Achar

Tangy mango pickle

Making time: 4-5 days

Ingredients:

Mangoes, raw, washed, cut into 1" pieces	5 kg
Salt	4 cups / 600 gm
Turmeric (*haldi*) powder	4 tsp / 16 gm
Fennel (*moti saunf*) seeds	200 gm
Fenugreek seeds (*methi dana*)	100 gm
Mustard seeds (*rai*)	6½ tbsp / 60 gm
Red chilli powder	15 tsp / 60 gm
Onion seeds (*kalonji*)	15 tsp / 30 gm
Black salt (*kala namak*)	15 tsp / 60 gm
Ginger powder (*sonth*)	10 gm
Cumin (*jeera*) seeds, roasted, powdered	6½ tsp / 10 gm
Garam masala	5 tsp / 10 gm
Asafoetida (*hing*)	½ tsp / 2 gm

Method:

1. Mix 2 tsp salt and 2 tsp turmeric powder with the mangoes. Keep overnight in a basket to drain out the water.

2. Spread the mangoes on a dry cloth, and sun-dry for 2-3 days.

3. Roast and pound the fennel seeds, fenugreek seeds, and mustard seeds coarsely. Mix with the remaining spices. Add to the mangoes and mix thoroughly.

4. Again keep the mango mixture in the sun for 4-5 days. Stir the pickle often and ensure that there is no moisture left.

5. When ready, store in airtight jars. This pickle stays good all the year round.

Kairia Achar

Tangy kairi *and mango pickle*

Preparation time; 15 min.
Makes: 1 kg approx.

Ingredients:

Kairia (see p. 7), fresh, washed	500 gm
Mangoes, raw, medium	5
Mustard (*sarson*) oil	1 cup / 200 ml
Red chilli powder	2 tbsp / 8 gm
Aniseed (*saunf*), coarsely ground	2 tbsp / 8 gm
Yellow mustard powder	2 tbsp / 8 gm
Turmeric (*haldi*) powder	1 tbsp / 4 gm
Salt	2 tbsp

Method:

1. Dry the *kairia* on a piece of cloth till all the moisture is absorbed.
2. Coarsely grate the mangoes and squeeze out all the liquid.
3. In a large bowl, mix all the ingredients together and leave overnight to mature.
4. Store in a dry, airtight glass jars.

Badam Ka Seera
Almond pudding

Preparation time: 5 hrs.
Cooking time: 35-40 min.
Serves: 6-7

Desserts

Ingredients:

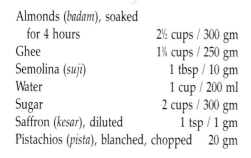

Almonds (*badam*), soaked
for 4 hours   2½ cups / 300 gm
Ghee   1¼ cups / 250 gm
Semolina (*suji*)   1 tbsp / 10 gm
Water   1 cup / 200 ml
Sugar   2 cups / 300 gm
Saffron (*kesar*), diluted   1 tsp / 1 gm
Pistachios (*pista*), blanched, chopped   20 gm

Method:

1. Peel and grind the almonds to a smooth paste.
2. Heat the ghee in a big wok (*kadhai*); add the semolina and almond paste; sauté on low heat for about 30 minutes.
3. When the paste becomes light brown, add the water and sugar; cook on high heat, stirring briskly for 4-5 minutes. The consistency should be semi thick and the texture should be soft.
4. Garnish with saffron and pistachios.

Churma

Crushed wheat flour cakes with pistachios

Preparation time: 25 min.
Cooking time: 20 min.
Serves: 8-10

Desserts

Ingredients:

Wholewheat flour (*atta*)	5 cups / 500 gm
Ghee	2 cups / 400 gm
Sugar, powdered	3 ²/₃ cups / 400 gm
Rock candy (*mishri*), small bit	50 gm
Saffron (*kesar*), diluted	1 tsp / 1 gm
Green cardamoms (*choti elaichi*), powdered	1 tsp / 2 gm
Pistachios (*pista*), blanched, chopped	50 gm
Rose water (*gulab jal*)	2 tsp / 10 ml

Method:

1. Sift the wholewheat flour; rub in 100 gm ghee and knead to a stiff dough.

2. Divide the dough equally into 20 balls and shape each into flat cakes.

3. Heat the remaining ghee in a wok (*kadhai*); slide the cakes, a few at a time, and fry on low heat till they are crisp and brown. Remove and repeat till all the cakes are fried. Keep aside to cool.

4. Pound the fried cakes and sift in a coarse sifter. Add the remaining ingredients; mix well together.

5. This can be served as it is or with *panchmela dal* (see p. 38) and *batti* (see p. 48).

Variations: *You can make small* laddus *with the* churma *by adding 2 tbsp ghee to the ready mixture.*

Kheer

Rich and creamy rice pudding

Preparation time: 30 min.
Cooking time: 40 min.
Serves: 6-7

Ingredients:

Milk	10 cups / 2 lt
Rice	1¼ cups / 125 gm
Sugar	1 ⅔ cups / 250 gm
Saffron (*kesar*), diluted in water	½ tsp / ½ gm
Almonds (*badam*), slivered	1¼ tsp / 20 gm
Pistachios (*pista*), slivered	1¼ tsp / 20 gm
Green cardamom (*choti elaichi*), powdered	¼ tsp

Method:

1. Wash the rice, drain excess water. Bring the rice and milk to a boil. Cook, stirring constantly, till the rice is tender and the milk is thick.
2. Add the sugar and cook for 10 minutes, stirring constantly. Remove from heat; add the saffron, almonds, pistachios, and green cardamom powder.
3. Serve hot or chilled.

Variation: *To make* kheeranand *double the quantity of rice mentioned. Fry rice in 2 tbsp ghee. Then add the milk, stir carefully on low heat so as not to break the rice. This preparation is thicker than* kheer *and tastes more like a rice pudding.*

Chena Parwal

Parwar stuffed with fresh cottage cheese

Preparation time: 45 min.
Cooking time: 30 min.
Makes: 8 pieces

Desserts

Ingredients:

Parwars (*parwal*), big, peeled,
  slit vertically, boiled, drained — 8
Sugar — 3 cups / 450 gm
Water — 1 cup / 200 ml
For the filling:
Fresh cottage cheese (*chena*) — 200 gm
Sugar, powdered — 1/3 cup / 50 gm
Almonds (*badam*), peeled,
  finely chopped — 8-10
Pistachios (*pista*), peeled,
  finely chopped — 10-12
Green cardamom (*choti elaichi*)
  powder — ½ tsp / 1 gm
Saffron (*kesar*), diluted in water — ½ tsp / ½ gm
Rock candy (*mishri*), small bits — 20 gm
Silver leaves (*varq*) — 2

Method:

1. Carefully remove the seeds from the parwars.
2. Boil the water and sugar together till the syrup is sticky. Add the parwars and cook on low heat, till the parwars change colour and become sweet.
3. **For the filling**, knead the cottage cheese with sugar, almonds, pistachios, saffron, green cardamom powder, and rock candy.
4. Drain the parwars, and fill each with the cottage cheese mixture. Press the filled parwars in your palm to give the original shape. Cover with silver leaves and serve.

Gond Ke Laddu

Sweet wheat flour balls

Preparation time: 2-3 hrs.
Cooking time: 30 min.
Makes: 16-17

Ingredients:

Gum raisin (*gond*) (available in
  dry fruit shops)   100 gm
Ghee   ¾ cup / 150 gm
Wholewheat flour (*atta*)   2½ cups / 250 gm
Almonds (*badam*), cut into
  3 horizontal pieces   100 gm
Sugar, powdered   250 gm

Method:

1. Break the gum raisin into small bits on a flat dish and sun for 2-3 hours.

2. Heat the ghee in a wok (*kadhai*); fry the gum raisin pieces till they double in size. Keep aside.

3. Strain the leftover ghee and reheat in a wok. Add the wholewheat flour, almonds, and sauté on low heat for approximately 20 minutes or till the flour is cooked.

4. Add the fried gum raisin pieces; mix well and keep aside to cool.

5. When cool, add the sugar, mix well and make about 15-16 small-sized balls. Store in airtight jars.

Pista Burfi
Pistachio squares

Preparation time: 20 min.
Cooking time: 15 min.
Makes: 10

Ingredients:

Green pistachios (*pista*), blanched	300 gm
Sugar	1 cup / 150 gm
Water	¾ cup / 150 ml
Saffron (*kesar*), diluted in	
½ tsp rose water	¼ gm
Silver leaves (*varq*)	2-3

Method:

1. Wipe the pistachios with a dry cloth and grind to a course paste.

2. Cook the sugar and water in a wok (*kadhai*) and bring to a boil. Keep stirring till the syrup becomes thick and is ready to set immediately. Remove from the flame.

3. Immediately add the pistachio paste. Mix well and transfer to a flat dish.

4. Grease your palms and knead the mixture into a soft dough. Flatten the dough on a greased table top. Roll it out carefully to make an ½"-thick square. Cover the entire square with the silver leaves.

5. With a sharp knife, cut the square into 1" small squares. Sprinkle the diluted saffron and serve.

Meetha Chawal

Sweetened rice

Preparation time: I hr.
Cooking time: 20 min.
Serves: 6

Desserts

Ingredients:

Basmati rice, soaked for 1 hour,
  drained   1¼ cups / 250 gm
Ghee   8 tbsp / 120 gm
Cloves (*laung*)   4
Green cardamoms (*choti elaichi*) 4
Cinnamon (*dalchini*), 1" stick 1
Sugar   2 cups / 300 gm
Saffron (*kesar*), soaked   1 tsp / 1 gm
Almonds (*badam*), blanched   25 gm
Pistachios (*pista*), chopped   25 gm
Pine nuts (*chilgoza*), peeled   25 gm

Method:

1. Parboil the rice and spread it out on a flat dish to cool.
2. Heat the ghee in a wok (*kadhai*); add the cloves, green cardamoms, and cinnamon stick.
3. Add ½ cup water, sugar, and saffron; stir till the syrup becomes slightly sticky.
4. Add the rice and stir carefully on low heat for 15 minutes or till the mixture is absolutely dry. Remove from heat.
5. Add the almonds, pistachios and tilgoza; mix gently. Serve hot.

Paneer Payas

Cottage cheese in thickened milk

Preparation time: 30 min.
Cooking time: 30 min.
Serves: 4-5

Desserts

Ingredients:

Milk	5 cups / 1 lt
Cottage cheese (*paneer*), grated coarsely	250 gm
Sugar	1 cup / 150 gm
Almond (*badam*) flakes	20 gm
Pistachio (*pista*) flakes	20 gm
Saffron (*kesar*), soaked in rose water	½ gm

Method:

1. Boil the milk till it thickens and is reduced to a quarter of the original quantity.
2. Add the sugar, mix well till it dissolves and keep aside to cool.
3. Add the cottage cheese and half the almond and pistachio flakes. Mix well.
4. Serve chilled, garnished with the remaining almond and pistachio flakes and saffron.

Aam Sandesh

Cottage cheese fudge stuffed with mango

Preparation time: 15 min.
Makes: 12-14

Ingredients:

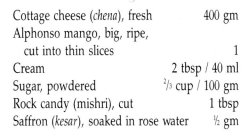

Cottage cheese (*chena*), fresh	400 gm
Alphonso mango, big, ripe, cut into thin slices	1
Cream	2 tbsp / 40 ml
Sugar, powdered	²/₃ cup / 100 gm
Rock candy (*mishri*), cut	1 tbsp
Saffron (*kesar*), soaked in rose water	½ gm

Method:

1. Squeeze the water out from the cottage cheese and mash well with your palms.
2. When it becomes soft and fluffy, add cream and sugar; mash well again.
3. Divide the mixture equally into 2 parts. Flatten the parts into ¼"-thick squares.
4. Cover the first square with the mango slices and then put the second layer over the mango, covering it completely.
5. With a broad knife, trim the edges neatly. Garnish with saffron and rock candy, and chill for at least ½ hour.
6. Cut into 1" squares and serve.

Suggested Menus

Snacks and Starters

Kanji (*Tangy mustard drink*) 10

Alu Sabudana Bara (*Fried potato and sago cakes*) 16

Vegetarian

Patli Mangori
(*Green gram pieces in tomato gravy*) 46

Kadhi (*Yoghurt and gram flour curry*) 42

Bharwan Parwal (*Stuffed parwar*) 36

Accompaniments

Bajre Ki Roti (*Millet flour bread*) 57

Gobi Matar Ke Chawal
(*Cauliflower and peas pilaf*) 60

Dessert

Badam Ka Seera (*Almond pudding*) 78

Snacks and Starters

Kesar Shikanji (*A refreshing saffron drink*) 14

Matar Gujiya (*Stuffed green pea patties*) 22

Vegetarian

Panchmela Dal (*Five-in-one pulse delight*) 38

Alu Bhujee (*Smoked potatoes*) 30

Gatte Ka Saag Dahiwala
(*Gram flour strips in yoghurt curry*) 41

Accompaniments

Batti (*Baked wheat flour bread dipped in ghee*) 48

Dahi Bhat (*Yoghurt rice with vegetables*) 63

Dessert

Churma
(*Crushed wheat flour cakes with pistachios*) 80

Glossary of Cooking Terms

Batter — A mixture of flour, liquid and sometimes other ingredients, of a thin or thick consistency.

Blend — To mix two or more ingredients thoroughly together.

Coat — To cover food that is to be fried with flour, egg and breadcrumbs, or batter.

Fry — To cook in hot fat or oil. In the case of shallow frying, only a small quantity of fat is used in a shallow pan. The food must be turned halfway through to cook both sides evenly. In the case of deep-frying, sufficient fat is used to cover the food completely.

Rub in — To incorporate the fat into flour, using the fingertips.

Sauté — To cook in an open pan in hot, shallow fat, tossing the food to prevent it from sticking.

Simmer — To boil gently on low heat.

Stir-fry — To fry rapidly while stirring and tossing.

Index

ISBN: 81-7436-245-2

© **Roli & Janssen BV 2002**
Published in India by
Roli Books in arrangement with
Roli & Janssen
M-75 Greater Kailash II (Market)
New Delhi 110 048, India
Ph: 6442271, 6462782, 6460886
Fax: (011) 6467185, E-mail: roli@vsnl.com
Website: rolibooks.com

Photographs: Sunny Singh

Printed and bound in Singapore